My Heavens

~

Harold Whit Williams

FUTURECYCLE PRESS
www.futurecycle.org

Cover photo and author photos by Ashley Savage Williams; cover and interior book design by Diane Kistner; PT Serif text and Shannon titling

Library of Congress Control Number: 2020930178

Published by FutureCycle Press
Athens, Georgia, USA

ISBN 978-1-942371-87-8

You grieve not that heaven does not exist
but that it exists without us.

—W. S. Merwin

In Memory of Betty Evelyn Williams
1941-2017

Contents

and night will be no more

in my father's house are many rooms

My Heavens

With the deepening darkness came rain
Rain with its despondent whisperings
Rain threading itself

Through the lowering sky, through
Leaves slumbering / Rain
Stitching itself into dreams

And dreadful imagery / Dreams
Disappearing as soon as they were dreamt
That sound of my breath a prayer

That clock on the wall wearing my face
At long last, it stopped
At long last, the rain slackened

Then stopped / The sky
Raised up on its haunches and howled
The whole world shuddered

And slunk back into its hole
Somewhere a pamphlet proclaimed
This was the first day of the rest of my life

One Man's Purgatory

And so it came to pass that nothing much happened.
Light and darkness and climate fluctuations.
Species evolving and a dance craze here and there.
The rains eventually falling, but mostly elsewhere

And of little consequence. I sang myself awake.
I could feel eternity like a pebble in my shoe.
I curled up inside that cabin of my soul

And awaited word from a world gone deaf and mute.
Sometimes a songbird in the dream out the window.
Sometimes a sunset that my mother would've loved.

All in all, it worked out fine. The ballet of leaves.
That bedtime story of shadows. My good ear
Cupped to the cold pane of midnight, almost catching
Some whispered secret from over the horizon.

Alabama Field Holler

Winter morning all hollowed out,
Whistling its one-note ballad.

Morning bark-stripped, sanded-down,
Held over a flame. A woodsmoke

Morning piping clear across
Back pastures of my childhood.

Let me wake early to cop the riffs
Of this bygone morning song.

Let me stomp out with snare drum
Past Granddaddy's electric fence.

I'll get in tune with morning, root
Myself down into the hard red clay.

I'll call a blues to myself in 4/4 time,
Stand back and await the response.

Tishomingo Still Life

A family picnics beside the sleeping river.
My family, your family, nobody's.
Thrift-store clothes, small-town haircuts.
Faces and gestures
Handed down through slumped-over years.
Midday summer sunlight
Singing cicada songs in the oaks,
In the loblolly pines.
Woodpecker drumming. Fishstink.
Yellowjackets on the icebox pie.
The river stirs, wakes, opens its one good eye.
A cloud passes, then another.
My or your or nobody's hands
Grapple for the smoothest stones to skip.
A half-dozen times or so.
They stone-sink into the silver current,
Rippling the water surface.
Rippled, time and space.
The river blinks, goes back to sleep.
The river dreams the family
Packing up for home.
The river has no beginning, no end.

First United Methodist Sutra

He leadeth me beside the still waters, I chanted as a child
From those cold pine pews of a yellow-brick church.
Corner of Main and Mythology. The sniffling,
The open casket, the waxy fallen face
Of some small-town elder.

But this is not a poem pinpricking the past,
Nor is it some cultural diatribe against my tribe—
Rather, a meditation upon the still waters,
Upon their metaphysical component
In the mumbled metaphor.

Water stilled, water silent, water held up
By its dark and murky depths.
And then the enlightened soul, the settled spirit,
Simply a pond's surface
Mirroring everything above and not above.

Never mind the stagnant shallows, the brittle reeds.
Never mind that stock-still egret poised
In his godless quest for the kill. Never mind
Who it was leading whom,
And wherever it was they were headed.

Render Unto Caesar

That big game long past, long lost.
The stadium filled with wind.

A multitude of lights left burning,
So bright they can be seen

By all the gods, myself included.
My songs unwritten. My hair

Grown long in dreams, in legends.
Let us slip through the parted curtains

Of this moment, fellow traveler.
Let us leave it all behind for others

To reconcile. Off-and-on rain showers
And the possibility of chance.

Sleepwalking. Metallurgy. Memory
Is a dollar-store jigsaw puzzle.

For They Know Not What They Do

Climbing down off this crooked crucifix
Once and for all.
Imagining my final cutting remark.
Mapping out my astral-projected getaway.
That low sky ossifying
Into an ashen gray. Cold, indifferent sky.
As a child, I drank magical river water
And spoke to Jehovah.
Now I quiver and cry in my sleep
Like some orphan.
I wake with fetal-position ache.
Those sheets retaining
The shape and scent of a ghost.
Risen from the dead for day-old coffee.
That bathroom mirror becoming
A stained-glass window.
Roll away the stone, sweet disbelievers,
And take my name in vain.

Euthanasia

For the most part, those days passed
Like migratory songbirds,
Never to be heard from nor seen again.
The medicine hitting its mark.
Those open wounds cauterized.
I had discovered a shadowy patch
Behind the apocalyptic library.
There I planted my nation's white flag
And waited for the press to show.
West wind almost rustling the leaves.
A towheaded boy
Dragging his little red wagon.
Taking copious notes, my alter ego
Discovered discrepancies
In the daylight-to-darkness ratio.
I figured as much.

For Your Consideration

Almost April and the grass summer-shimmers,
Greening in the afternoon.
Somewhere you read that your dreams
Are not relevant. Never were.
And just outside this cafe door, the universe
Is expanding, with or without you.
Mammatus clouds, bee-crowded blossoms,
A mockingbird mocking the ATM's beep.
So many surrogate mothers everywhere—
Why must you shuffle about
Like the proverbial orphan? You wipe
A single tear from a wrinkled cheek.
You pray a jet plane overhead.
A metal miracle filled with future angels
Chemtrailing this made-for-TV moment.
Possibly you know someone
On that plane. You see them in memory.
Wave up at them. Wave bye-bye.
Like memories, as each second passes
They are further and further beyond.

Unsteady Lines

Thunder me back from the murky edge of memory.
The schoolyard at false dawn,
The uncut grass flash-frozen. Dog-bitten
And damned beside the drought-dry creek.
A mouth filled with music.
A fever high from blood reckoning.

I believe dreams grow on the north side of trees.
I believe in someone else's time,
In someone else's weather.
I believe in a deity unbelievable,
Raking us all over the coals
To prove some pointless point.

What a strange smoke scent this morning,
And I keep trying your number.
Just the sound of lapping water, of perch
Popping in shallows.
Throw out the lifeline, throw out the lifeline—
Someone is slipping away.

Bicameralism in Lauderdale County

Today is a day like another day I remember:
Sky slightly askew—half-blue, half-gray—
Faintest waft of factory smoke,
Soft rock on AM radio.
Mother driving us home with groceries.
Seeing my imaginary friend

Jump off the Tennessee River Bridge.
He was a he and I spoke to him at night.
I was nine. I needed glasses.
I watched his imaginary body float past,
Headed for Waterloo, for Pickwick,
For Shiloh. He looked like me

Without a face. He forgave my sins, whatever
They were. He dove headfirst into
The churning water. We would've stopped
To fish him out, to bury him, but
I was already second-guessing myself,
And there were perishables in the back seat.

Vignette for Frank O'Hara

The Indian summer afternoon was bleeding out
On its flat-earth stretcher
With no hope of resuscitation,
With no priest for last rites.
And something about that play of light

Slanting through yellowing leaves
Made me want to ouija board my grandmother
For folksy instructions on canning,
On preserving the last of the season's okra,
Field peas, squash and peppers.

But my workmate was before me,
Swirling her worries around inside a coffee cup,
So I found myself listening to
But not really hearing whatever it was she sang.
It sounded like verse/chorus/algorithm.

It changed keys into a bee's drone.
It slow-faded to some commercial break
For new cars and trucks with no money down.
Then the weather report and its magical realism—
More of the same, more of the same.

Last Lunch Poem for Frank O'Hara

After the cafeteria meatloaf special, I find myself
Beneath an oak emptied of pigeons,
An oak filled with wind gusts,
And I recall waking from a dream
Or dreaming from a wake.
There I am beside Mother's open casket.
She is laughing and vivacious,
Her hair lustrous, her complexion ruddy.
I try to interject, to ask—
You know that you are dead, right?
But then the alarm issues its ultimatum,
And I lie there inside this tomb of Tuesday flesh,
Memorializing myself for five more minutes.
And later on I message my living sister.
She is invisible behind her screen.
She sends some funny-fonted reply—
Jealous of your spirit visitation,
Knowing it was wasted on a godless grouch—
O how she yearns for contact from Beyond!
So I paste in links for Jung and for Saigyō,
Then hobble off to the men's room
To rid myself of this holy water.

Broken Arrow

Such an utter mystery, this day-after-day.
Dog alarms, cars barking,
Oak pollen upon the blank page.

Jet planes arcing from nowhere to anywhere.
Sweet surreptitious sighs
From wet root and vine. Clouds

Like monks on the mountain path of sky.
Why, oh why these gnats
In my backyard whiskey? The afternoon

Floating facedown in a golden ennui.
Every day a holy day to anticipate,
To religiously observe.

The transubstantiation, the utter mystery.
I swallow it all
And expect nothing in return.

I believe in the zero sum of Before + After.
I believe in daylight on the windowsill.
I believe another drink is in order.

I salute whatever part of my soul that still wanders:
Pontotoc, Winnemucca, Thrall,
Broken Arrow. That little piece of my soul

Fixing a flat outside of Fort Worth.
The south wind whispering its one promise
In the greening prairie grass.

Missing Inclement Weather On a Sunny Afternoon

The sky intoxicatingly blue. Sky gone
Payday drunk, tipsy
With its own sense of the infinite,

With its own
Weightless heft. And just last week
Those low clouds conspired

To keep us all hunkered down,
Shoe-gazing,
Scurrying like ants from shelter to shelter.

I hid in my room for days, jotting notes
In Esperanto, shuffling about
With tissue-box-slippered feet.

All the while,
That biblical rain spoke in tongues I could
Almost understand.

Sounded like idle threats in old ballad form.
Sounded like Earth's epitaph
Recited in Babylonian. The telephone

Became my silent partner,
The grocery list an epic poem.
I had never felt so alive.

Incidental Music

A low hum in the background of everything.
Low hum and the click track of hours.
I pan myself to the left, then right.
I pull the faders on a long workday.

Satie and his snuff box. His long fingernails.
Bo Diddley and that loaded pistol
On the passenger seat.
All hits. No filler.

The world plays out in mono.
The world demands its guarantee up front.
Both sides of my brain backstage, muted.
There will be no encore.

Summer Sunday Chance Music

I have dreamt this day before, with its
Ticking parlor clock, with its
Stifling sun-hot breezeless purgatory.

What's needed is a folk song, an aria,
Or just pie and coffee.
What's needed is more of the same.

More of the same. Same shorts
And T-shirt. Same
Shuffling sandals. Same

Shameless headlines and bylines
Swerving our psyches
To and fro. *I've got a home in Gloryland,*

Granddaddy sang, and I suppose
Daddy still does.
He has dreamt his summer Sundays

As well; sun-hot, breezeless. My photo
Recurring in all rooms.
A figment, an idea, a child of God.

Gnossienne No. 1

Such shadows cast upon the meadow
Of my heart. Westerlies flattening
The sage grass. Wind and shadows.
The meadow of my heart.

Afternoon elongating, growing out
Like a dead composer's fingernails.
Afternoon becoming minor key, atonal,
Becoming avant-garde. Afternoon

Becoming dissonant, diffident.
Black keys and white keys
Side by side in the graveyard.
Sunset coda. Sustain pedal lets up.

Cataclysmia In G Major

A day like no other, except for all of them.
A day unable to mourn its own passing.
The air closing ranks around us.

Those molecules with their secret launch codes.
Stone Age relics in the backyard
Just beneath the substrata of my indifference.

I have my coffee and my sweet things.
I pace up and down the hall in a measured fashion
Looking for something that isn't there.

An aboriginal song looping in my head.
The one without a chorus.
The one that keeps the world from ending.

Blue Norther

Such muted music of overnight weather.
The heart's metronome slowing,
Largo, largo. Such lackluster litanies,
Such a cacophony of thought.

A harvest moon gone jaundiced.
Trees talking in their sleep.
I am at one with nothing,
Neither nothingness nor somethingness.

I am scratching and clawing
At the storm windows of myself. I am
Staring down the hall
Into Mother's room. Her journals,

Her jewelry, her hair on the pillow.
A light that we see
We think we see. It soon enough fades,
And we forget.

All the Way Home

Our future selves in a field of sky.
A field of light, a field of electrons.
Here we are. There we were.
Whatever was dreamt absorbed.

Whatever was left of darkness absorbed.
Everything expanding
At a rate of something to something.
Nothing lasts forever and only nothing.

The dance is set to begin. The dance
Of no remembrance.
The dance of light and electrons.
Of this, I am almost certain.

Colbert Mountain Sutra

We wake all of a sudden beside the dream's fire.
Smoke-shrouded, moon-haunted.
Dream of the dreamless,

Dream of bones and hair. The fire
Of what's-to-come.
The fire of whatever-will-be.

The fire moon-haunted and all of a sudden.
We hem and haw; we till our bloodless soil.
We thumb rides

Along some celestial highway.
Riven, our words, our shallow deeds.
Riven and tattered

At the charred end of a hard day.
O for a thousand tongues to sing,
They sang and they sung,

And it stung our memories
Like bees after first frost, like static
From the pump, like love

Before the loss of love.
This old world, the weight of a stone,
And all that we know

And think that we know,
As inconsequential as an eyelash
On my sleeping mother's pillow.

Epiphany in D Minor: The Saddest of All Keys

It was all a bit different this time around.
The cafe, the coffee, those hominids
Sitting next to me. And the sizes,
The shapes of various rain puddles.
The wind most certainly not whispering.

Staccato grackle-squawk in fast 9/8.
Those schoolchildren outside the museum
Oddly quiet, their wizened little faces
Scrunched up in past-life pain.
Friends and family, truth be told,

Still friends and family, but altered
Remarkably at the molecular level.
Like online photos tinted sepia
For sappy effect. I, of course, was
Rock-of-Gibraltaring my way

Through all of this. Haunting
That old corner table, scrawling
Future police sketches of everyone,
Eavesdropping for the good
Of our nation. And then it hit me.

they will need no light of lamp nor sun

My Heavens

Lie just beyond the snowfences
Beyond that far ridge
Where vision fails and falls to stones
An aspen leaf, a raindrop
A swallow stunned and stilled in flight

My heavens a string quartet, a trumpet blast
A field holler by a bend in the river
My heavens exotic, entrancing
A sip of aguardiente
In some palm-lined courtyard

My heavens dreamt but not discussed
Sung but not studied
A fib, a fact, a muttered half-truth
A full moon glimpsed atop the skyscraper
That last swig of sundown wine

Stranger In a Strange Land

Tossed in sleep like a man lost at sea.
Awakened
To another unmapped island of a day.
Odd squawks of babbling blackbirds.
A subtropical
Sun toasting my tender skin.

Some strange whispering patois of wind
In tall grass, in leaves,
Leaving me speechless, disoriented,
Unsure of what to do next.
Just keep spinning in space, no doubt.

Just keep plotting coordinates,
Jotting down field notes.
Just keep bringing bright beads and baubles
To that fearsome native tribe.
Their dialect indecipherable; their
Customs beautiful and frightening.

Apropos of Nothing

Feeling like death warmed over,
I discuss Dickinson with a coworker
And swear I hear a fly buzz.
Some kind of racket going on here.
Some play of light
Early in the day, early in the year.
Sky smeared white, sky postmodern
And over itself.
I'm playing possum in the supply closet.
I'm searching for something
Beyond the breakroom window.
I'm rubbing two coins together
And reciting the state pledge backwards.
And just over the horizon,
Halfway to heaven,
Daddy nods off in his recliner.
His hands two mourning doves
At roost. His face a mask
Bathed in the orange glow
Of televised atrocities. His dreams
Becoming more and more real.

What are the Odds?

Still wagering with this ghost inside me
That our shadowy old world
Cannot last much longer.

Another morning steaming deep
Inside the cracked cup.
Another dream left at the curb.

This ghost inside clawing to get out,
Chicken-scratching for forever.
This ghost adored

For his manifestations, his expressions,
His primitive art scrawled
Upon the cave walls of my ego.

And this tired husk finds itself at times
Beyond clouds, sipping soda
Beneath the blue edge of heaven.

Hedging bets from a turbulence prayer.
A skeleton seen within the stewardess.
All engines fail eventually.

Love Thy Neighbor

Indian summer clouds skirting my sky again.
Watch me slow time.
Watch me slow time and reverse it.

Some parlor trick, this. Some smoke
And mirrors bliss.
Daylight as a tincture

Filling up my empty wineglass.
I sip from it yet feel no effect.
And the towheaded boy I am becoming

With a pasture of sadness inside his heart
Still seeks something
Beyond randomness, beyond chaos.

Hear his timid knock upon the side door.
See his hands shake
Holding up the empty cup for sugar.

King Harvest Has Surely Come

Another holiday here within Berryman's warm walls.
Ancestral intuition, incense of sage and rosemary.
Sacrament of late morning light upon the oaks,
Upon the cactus pads and uncovered grill.
Other side of way over there,

The old family home sits empty as the Lord's tomb,
Resting among cold pines by a bend in the river.
Best not to think too much about it.
Best not to question the Void and its intentions.
Sure, intone and beseech, send up little prayers

Like smoke signals from a Saturday western.
The cornucopia fills with days and weeks and years
Dried and yellowed from time's fever.
Hold hands, beg grace.
The reply comes, silent and endless.

Raking Leaves Near the Winter Solstice

Inside the afternoon's dream I pause to recall
A line from Basho:
Poetry is a fireplace in summer or a fan in winter.

And then another, from Huddie Ledbetter:
I may be right and I may be wrong.
You know you're gonna miss me when I'm gone.

Such is the penance bones and flesh pay
For the privileges of pleasure/pain
And the passage of time.

The rake, the leaves, my self
Within my body.
The dream within this afternoon's dream.

And the season employs me.
The Chinese tallow, the red oak, employ me.
No payday scrip, no company store—

Just the blood-orange sunset for recompense,
Just the smoke-tinged air. A wind
Filling next year's coffers with nothing.

Cautionary Tale

Whatever was dreamt drew down the rain.
It rained like a lover's whisper.
It rained and kept things to itself.
It rained like the neighbor boy crying
On the other side of the fence.

It rained like Mother said it did in 1947.
And whatever was dreamt
Does not matter. No koan, no sutra
Beyond wind in the leaves, beyond waves
At the shore. This is not about dreams.

This is not about the weather.
This is not about the pen dancing
With the blank page, synapses
Firing upon helpless women and children.
This is not about

Little Bear Creek outside of its banks,
The bridge washed out, those crops lost.
This is about bones and breath,
Meat and muscle. This is about what happens
When one wakes up.

Tishomingo Sutra

Cicada drone blue-sky dharma afternoon.
Everything beginning to fade around the edges.
Everything going the way of the old family farm.
All shadowed stories and hearsay.
Hushed chatter from the back pews.
I still climb those pines of childhood
For a far-off glimpse of future,
For that suggestive caress of oblivion's breeze.
My speech has become sticky with sap,
Untranslatable and in love with itself,
My heart some folded road map
Misshelved in the hometown library.
Eyes on the prize. Hands across America.
There is no pond without its reflection.
There is no going without the return.

High Harmony

Evening filling up the sky like a river rising
In the lock of a dam.
My heart risen to my throat. My heart
A barge heavy with necessities,
With frivolities and the like.

Those old folks long gone.
Their shape notes long gone.
Whole years pass by like parades
No one heard about.

I could sit out on my back steps
To empty a bottle and count the miles
Between lightning and thunder.
I could insist that the world
Follow me down a dead-end road.

Instead, I stay inside
With Grandmother's quilts
And her rusted knives,
Not believing a word the radio says.

Everybody Do the Mesozoic

Absence of the crow in an oak's bare branches.
Absence of rain in a hungover sky.

Duly noted, transcriber of nothing,
Watcher in the woods, gad about town.

All these bones dancing around us.
All these long shadows longing for home.

Someday soon a song might suggest otherwise,
But I have absolute faith

In geologic time. In the tick-tock
Drip-drop upon flint, upon schist and granite.

Hear my prayers, seismic shift.
Have mercy upon me, chemical chance.

Never Enough to Go Around

High holy processional of thin cirrostratus,
Of cumulonimbus and chemtrails.

Sunlight turns itself down a notch.
Wind dies alone atop some faraway hill.

Even birds ground themselves,
Hushed in supplication.

I take to the city streets like a stray dog
On any Sunday.

Last year's gutter leaves. Memory's detritus.
This fellow on my bus

Holding his own against the gods,
Against time and space,

Against the nature of being.
I blink once and the world has changed.

I change my mind
And the world stays the same.

Without Knowing Why, He Followed

After Barry Hannah

Somebody hollering in the Delmar Baptist Church.
Hollering meat and muscle. Hollering heaven.

Somewhere, the Lord is walking
With a limp and a cane.

He's down the wrong side of the road
Waking up coon dogs.

He's in the middle of a cemetery at midnight.
Confederate stillborns. Oak stumps.

Poison sumac around the edges of everything.
His bottle gone empty, the morning

A lifetime away. His night sky
Just sheet music no one can sight-read.

Spruce Pine Mountain Solstice

Just at the edge of memory's back pasture,
The sun-dappled grass,
The meadowlark on a fence.

Day moon like some white man's god
Pierced by a chemtrail
On the late afternoon's cross.

Whatever's left of this season shuffled off
And gusting about
By the side of Old Memphis Highway.

I'm chewing on the cud of this year.
Standing dumb and still,
Chewing, chewing.

I'm ruminating in lengthening shadows,
Shadows lengthening
From that copse of oaks on a nearby knob.

And where is Mother? And where
Is her mother?
Where,

If not here in the sun-dappled grass.
Where, if not here
In the tiny heaven of the mind.

More Unsteady Lines

The morning wakes with vertigo, with a sudden
Spinning inevitability. Morning
Harrowed, hungover
From getting tight the night before.
Morning tilted towards a light in the distance.
Leaning, morning is,
Leaning on the everlasting arms.

Six weeks have passed; still I find myself
Thinking to call. Our Sunday talks now daily
And thoroughly metaphysical.
You, repurposed in an undiscovered astral plane.
You, inhabiting the future
In some space we cannot measure yet.
You, incredibly, ho-hummedly vanished.

And I am simply demarcating the quotidian,
The mathematics of it all.
I am continuing our conversations
With the You inside my graying matter.
I, more alone, more aloof,
Cutting-and-pasting this middle-aged corpus
Into whatever it is

That passes for existence.
Morning, of course—always another morning.
The spinning inevitability of sky,
Of time. Harrowed. Hungover.
Time tilted towards some light in the distance.
That soft tick of the chisel
As it nicks another day's headstone.

Umbilical

A storm forming on the other side of the river.
Some storm like a simile
But the river literal.

Winds whitecapping the water,
And I am a child.

I am a child as the sky turns biblical.
I am a child born of rain and cosmic dust.

Long before Old Testament God,
There was wind and water
And the other side of the river.

There was the child I am
And the child I am becoming.

There was the beginning and the end.
There was no excuse for what came next.

Beatitude

Back in the days before God left me,
He and I would walk hand-in-hand
Like sweethearts at recess

Beneath his patented blue sky,
Beneath his little clouds
Of cherubim and seraphim.

That strong, silent type, God.
His rugged jawline, his forever eyes,
The way he knew exactly what was coming.

I donned my hair shirt
And acted accordingly. I sang tenor
On the old country hymns.

I kept each unanswered prayer
And pondered them all in my heart.
After awhile, it got easier,

Those long walks alone. Hands forgotten
In pockets, a biting north wind,
The sky gone gray and uninterested.

It was as if I had died
And been born again. It was as if
He had never even existed.

Pass/Fail

Sometimes there is a shadow within shadows.
The end of a dark hallway
And nothing more.

This haunting of head voices,
These remnants of dreams
Like scraps of cloth across the face.

We see the past in field glasses
Hovering high like some bird of prey.
We hear grass grow, soil settle.

We shiver from the chill of someone else's tomb,
Our names and places
Wiped from that schoolhouse map.

Thunder in the distance,
The playground empty.
This will all be on the test.

Vacation Bible School 1974

Bright rooms in the back of the mind
Wallpapered with watercolors,
With finger smudges.

Jesus loves me. Jesus wept.
The afternoon climbs down
Off its crucifix. The afternoon

Rolls away the stone and saves itself.
God's green grass
And the manna of chewing gum.

Hot sun upon the sidewalk,
And I cry for the arms of Mother.
Something about heaven.

Something about transubstantiation
And the Holy Ghost. I weep.
I cry for green heaven to this very day.

Indian Mound Field Trip 1976

The river leads us to a place of bones.
Warriors, women, holy men and infants.
Our childhands tremble, our childvoices quiver

Lacking the arrows of ancient song.
Chickasaw sediment beneath our childfeet.
Dead grass adorned with blood-red leaves.

I smell their blood to this very day.
I hear the river shushing us
While on the other side of town

Someone trades places with his shadow.
Other side of this memory,
The highway snakes out of its skin.

Our childbodies leave us beside the river.
For the first and last time,
The river changes its mind.

Keeping Vigil

There is a light in the grass the dead leave on for us.
I've seen it at dusk beneath mountain laurel blossoms.
Sad-sack sun sinking, and that light left on
Glowing in greening grass. I've seen it at dawn

In surprise frost, crystal-glistening the tiny blades.
My breath like cloud prayers. My bones
Cold as the grave. Too much the dead are with us,
Yet too little sway they hold. The dead fretting,

The dead pacing, the dead staying up late
As we dance and thumb our noses at curfew.
I, for one, will leave the dead be at long last.
It's the very least I can do, until I can do no more.

Hawk Pride Mountain Sutra

Lie down, stray dog of the ego. Lie down
Beside this fire of nevermind.
Lie down and know
That I was once invisible,

Invisible as Christ on a Saturday night.
Memory in reverse.
Virga on the weather radar.
I was dreamt by Mother
In that shouting church down the holler.

Dreamt by Daddy
Before he slipped off the bluff.
Dreamt by sister on her quarter horse
In the sun. The sun like a god

And the dream like a vision.
Lie down, little vision,
In the winter field of this page.
Make your snow angel, sweetheart.
Make your mark to melt, then move on.

Caught by the Indian Summer Train

I keep missing the exit for that hometown in my mind.
The borough in broken pieces
Scattered on the other side of the tracks.

They're waiting up for me, I know,
Fretting, hand-wringing,
Frittering about the fried pie table.

That porch light with its congregation of moths.
That harvest moon like a Buddha
Atop yonder ridge.

The leftovers. The folded quilts.
Those sepia ghosts in their dollar-store frames.
Evening deepening,

Sinking down to get comfortable.
A lone dogwood hunkering up against the house.
It leaves little flames flickering,

Its afterglow some sort of metaphor
For the fire we return to,
For the ashes sprinkled upon our slumbers.

and night will be no more

My Heavens

Far too much blue sky on pages and above
Too many harps not in clouds
Too many streets unpaved with gold

The trumpet shall not sound
The angel shall not appear
Far too much beyond love and whatever lies

Beyond Beyond / Far too often I stray
To pray any way that I can
With pen, with pad, with plucked

Dead string daydreams / My heavens
My heavens begin and end all around me
My holy face up low and high in rain

In the stained glass window of a city bus
All these little heavens of every day
All these little sometime salvations

Traffic wildflower emergency meditations
Take what you are given, image of god
Driven to death, we live almost forever

Peacenik

It all starts coming into focus: the new leaves,
The baby doves, that manifest destiny
Of afternoon traffic.
Everything begins to make a bit of sense:
The hushed cafe chatter,
The cash register's coded beeps,
That delivery truck gunning it
Outside the war museum. My shadow and I
Share a sun-splashed window table,
Taking an inventory
Of past and future grudges.
I'm saving a seat for some alternate reality.
I'm cozying up to whatever's not there.
My shadow burns his draft card,
Says he has other plans. He says
We will never get this moment back. He says
We barely had it to begin with.

Suburban Ephemera

I have a degree from the university of oblivion
and I'm as empty-handed as the shirt on the clothesline.
—Tomas Tranströmer

Wonders upon wonders other side of this windowpane.
I cannot explain nor deny them.

Clouds begin their mysterious journeys.
An anole gray on the photinia's trunk.

Butterflies like solar flares drip-dropping among tropical flowers.
Flowers gaudily colored as if by a sightless child savant.

The palm tree swaying, writhing.
Puffed air cooing through the dove's throat pouch.

I crack the window to hear mown grass chant its single-note mantra.
I sit back as thunder rattles the spoon in its coffee cup.

This chair holds my frame.
This frame holds my heart.

This heart has a door that's been slowly opening for years.
Down the hall I can see that there's nothing yet to see.

Gnostic Poem for Maurice

I am almost ready to catch fire and pray.
Almost done with mystery,
Almost fatigued by this flat-tire fate.

I am almost river, almost red clay,
Almost that song sung
By the side of Mother's grave.

And what a beautiful hoax: forever.
What a slight-of-hand,
This late-winter afternoon. The air

Like a lover's breath, blush
Of redbud blossoms, green parakeets
Squawking on the power line.

Everything simpatico with the sense
Of its senselessness. Everything
Inhabiting its own preposterous heaven.

Pistols at Dawn

Heavenless shards of morning sky.
Homeless the self on this sunlit stoop.
Strange how the clouds
Have disassembled—

They have gone to meet their maker.
They will dwell forever
In Paradise. Traffic hum. Dove murmur.
Pistols at dawn for my ego and me.

I am going for broke with both eyes closed,
One hand tied behind my back
In the game of life. Twenty paces barefoot
In the grave-cold grass

And I turn to trigger. I draw a blank.
My heart takes such shrapnel
And makes room for more. My heart
Beats on like a soldier's drum.

Homesick Ballad in C Minor

Tuned and plucked by the plectrum of time.
Opening riff of west wind
Rattling the high tupelo branches.

Bobwhite. Whippoorwill. Low hills
Wreathed in woodsmoke.
Slow music of rain upon the singing river.

A theme develops from the formless form:
Fencepost hawks, barbed wire down,
Patterns in the quilt on a dead woman's bed.

Thunder takes a solo. Last verse, last chorus.
One time I lay in a summer pasture
And watched the sky become itself.

Provisional Seismic Readings

Hauling my bones to the other side of nowhere.
Measuring the density of my own star-stuff.
Positively Precambrian,

This overcast afternoon. Late Jurassic,
That crow-and-grackle soundtrack.
Strange rumblings

In the substrata of dreams, aftershocks
Quivering the day-old coffee. Science
Can take us or leave us. Science

Proves us wrong day-in, day-out. Science
Finds us before the fridge at 4 a.m.,
Replenishing cell structure

And scrounging around for cold cuts. All hail
Science and its white flag of indifference.
All hail that hungry something

Scratching outside the archives door.
Let us pause here, bookmark our spot,
And invite that thing inside.

Song of the Übermensch

Another day, another shovelful of clay
Clodded upon
That six-feet-under psyche, upon

The Id, the Ego, the Chinese *qi*.
Dearly beloved,
We are gathered here today

Beneath that blue-sky heaven
Of ordinary moments. Only a step
To the grave, Grandmother sang,

And yet here I am
With my parakeets, with my sunshine,
Tequila solar-flaring

My nervous system. Here I am
Wadding up world news
To light the grill, still laughing

At a coworker's joke, the punchline's
Green bananas
And preprogrammed cell death.

Oblivion Devotional

That wind in the sage grass a kind of prayer.
The observance of, another kind.

Some idea of God
In the wind, in the roots and shadows.

God on his little throne
In the backs of everyone's minds.

I left God by the side
Of Old Memphis Highway.

He needed a shave and a room to let.
He needed someone to call his own.

Objects in the rearview mirror
Appear more irrelevant than they are.

Ideas, figments, fragments
In the great cosmic puzzle. I resist

The temptation to find deep meaning
In the quotidian.

I object, Your Honor,
To my whole line of questioning.

Never who, what, where or when,
But always why.

Pretty Mouth

Hung upside down in an old sweetgum.
Hogtied. Bend of the river
Autumn. Almost frost.

Bled out by those workweek wounds,
By those little day-in/day-out barbs.
Tried to ask for a last cigarette

But could only snort
And whinny, could only chomp
These molars. What's left of my spirit

Gutted, tossed to those blueticks
Yowling by the fire.
Hogtied, bled out and gutted, eyes

Open to the lidless sky. I thought death
Would just be darkness, but it's
More akin to the color of woodsmoke.

Fifteen Minutes in Heaven

On your state employee-mandated break time,
Visit the charming courtyard
To sit in and doze off on bright winter afternoons.
Sunlight warming the benches and chairs,
Filling up the space
Between buildings. Buildings rearing up
Into endless blue.
Passing cumulus puffed up
Like baby-fat cherubs, like obese angels.
And don't bother with a book
Or coffee,
Just bring the Self to lose through nonthinking.
O potted perennials!
O sugar ants filing forth!
Leafless trees starting to stir and sap,
Each falling drop sparkling like an ice pellet.
From the nearby clock tower
An hour chimes.
A peregrine falcon shrieks.
That's your shadow there on the pavement
Begging you to stay forever.

Lines For a Friend Halfway Crossed Over

Late summer leaves trembling, slight sway
Of silver branches.
A single cirrus cloud—apprehensive, tail-tucked—
Scurrying across all that mystic blue.
Something indefinable
Lingering in the air like woodsmoke.
Something unspeakable coming down the pike—
Something vast, incomprehensible.
You don't have to tell me twice, mister.
I'm the one navel-gazing, tea sipping,
Pacing the floor with pen and pad.
I'm that man-child at the window,
Method acting, waving hello/goodbye
To each passing moment. And I cannot
For the life of me
Remember the last time we spoke. Speak
When spoken to. Phonemes. Inflections.
Banished from heaven on a day like today.
Sometimes I feel like a motherless child.
Sometimes I something someplace or other.
Somewhere a hymnal
Falls from its piano, pages opening
To "The Old Rugged Cross." Let some
Bywater brass band march us all home to that one,
Our pine boxes bedazzled
And shimmering in the Delta sun.

Ornithology 101

A rude north wind spring morning. A blackberry
Winter morning. A baby bird of a morning.

Today sits peeping on the edge of its nest.
Today has its beak wide open, waiting

For whatever the world might shove down it.
As a child, I kept a fledgling

Brown thrasher in a Keds shoebox
In the washroom. Daddy dug up worms

And grubs to pamper it for days,
And I soon came to resent all that attention,

All that nurturing he gave the little bastard.
I know that time makes orphans of the lot of us,

But that cold wind today is the reason
I'm telling you this. Also, my teeth ache.

My back aches. And these shoulders ache
Where my wings should be.

Incidental Water Music

Why not return to those sweet streams of adolescence?
There is no one here to stop us. No one at all.
The garden hose, the swimming pool,

That cattle pond dragonfly-dotted. Granddaddy's
Chaparral creek
Swollen and somber with late winter rains.

I find myself often at a bend in the dream's river.
I find myself lost
Along the banks of these blank pages.

There is something to water besides life
And its elements. Something
Beyond death, and it reflects among the reeds.

I am thirsty for the past but I keep drinking future,
The present
Flowing fast inside a riptide of others.

There is something to water and the memory
Of water. I keep coming up for air
But forgetting to breathe.

Old Time Religion

I want a poem I can grow old in. I want a poem I can die in.
—Eavan Boland

Can't seem to recall that last conversation
But take comfort in the fact
That our mother/son voices beamed out

Into the heavens,
Then back down into each other's ears.
Voices of the heavens. Heavenly voices.

I pick up the receiver now and again
For time and for temperature,
For telekinesis and wrong numbers.

I cup my ear to the morning mirror
And catch myself in a familiar lie.
I drift off on occasion

To the church music of meadowlarks.
They are piping in that old pasture
Where the coon dogs are buried.

There was, and is, and will be eternity.
I believe in it now
Because I've heard it singing.

Catoctin River Meditation

A long woodland night laden with dreams
Of dubious portent, heavy
With visions gusted in on northwesterlies
Off the Alleghenies.
But morning now, clearing. A sky
Clean and cold. October
With its proverbs, with its minor-key
Murder ballads. October
Baring its fangs and growling like a cur.
Allegheny wind
Tuvan throat-singing in the eaves,
And I'm listening
For those notes between the notes.
I'm scanning that half-stripped maple
For signs and wonders,
For pieces of the Great Puzzle. O maple,
You crooked-branched harbinger,
Your sweet sap is slowing
And for once I'm in sync. O crow,
You strange traveler,
You drop of midnight on the patchwork
Quilt of trees, barbaric-yawp me
Back to that childhood pasture, the one
Awaiting my ashes
And the ashes of my memories.

Bear Creek Meditation

Forget your first and last name, forget the boat.
Forget the banks tangled with sumac.
Forget goldfinch song

And family. Forget purpose and oblivion.
Breathe clear the awful indentured mind
Like some daydreamt summer sky.

Unhook each caught thought
And return them all to their cold currents.
Follow this flow. Let go of intentions. There is

No boat for thoughts. No purpose
For oblivion. Just the sun-bright water.
Just the honeysuckle taste of this moment.

Boxing Day Blacktop Meditation

Driving that early morning highway—
North Mississippi, Natchez Trace,

Belmont then Tupelo,
French Camp then Kosciusko—

South by southwest away
From holiday clatter and clutter,

Away from small-minded chatter
And small-town horizons.

Please open your hymnal to page 237.
Let earth receive her king.

All is calm, all is bright.
It seems we've lost sight, they say,

Of the true meaning
And I, for once, agree: whatever meaning

We thought we had in our sights
Bounding off

Like that roadside buck,
His white-flag fanny flashing,

Topping the barbed-wire fence,
Disappearing into a slash pine thicket.

That Memphis station gone static.
My mind a field of unmarked snow.

Half-Assed Meditation After Reading Revelations

Let someone else make it rhyme.
—Stephen Dunn

Drawing nigh, this time of reckoning,
This time of so much to answer for,

Or not so much, or possibly
Nothing at all. Breathe in, breathe out;

Not sure what this could be about,
And the day/night sky is of no use.

Cries for help? Supplications?
They bounce right off of it to land

Like dime-store marbles in the lawn.
I run them over with my mower

To ding up the neighbor's car. Suffering,
Impermanence. Blah blah blah.

Breathe in, breathe out; Jesus returns
Singing "Twist and Shout."

Think I'll quit this wannabe city
With its teenage crush upon itself.

Think I'll stop considering sky, writing
About sky, writing beneath sky,

Or considering skywriting. Think I'll
Leave things here and pick up tomorrow.

The Past Isn't Even Past Pastoral

Shadows lengthening across Father's face.
An autumn sun setting behind his eyes.
Speak once again of the family farm—
That old clapboard house

Hidden from the highway,
The tornado's path still traced
By split trunks, bottomland cotton

Curving alongside Bear Creek.
The arrowheads, the slop jars,
Those stubble fields set fire to.
Bobwhite quail whistled up

On a morning not unlike this one,
With smoke in the wind
And a hymn hummed inside the heart.

Highway 43 Revisited

Autumn again by a bend in the river.
Dry grass, leaf scatter,
And the hush of songbirds. Hillsides
Huddled up, quilted for the coming frost.

Strange how it all circles back to the narrative,
But there sits Daddy
In his lawn chair, sucking his teeth,
Worrying up a prayer for Mother.

She is surely not satisfied
With her resting place by the highway.
The truck noise, the exhaust fumes,
Hillbillies gunning it from one sin to the next.

The sky is ashen and respectful enough,
And those funereal cedars
Do soften the senses, but this old road
Has already moved on

And forgotten her. It stretches before us,
Gray and godless.
Just another reminder of where she came from,
Of where she ended up.

Bend of the River Sutra

Before long the sky goes gray and lowers,
Manifesting past and all skies
Low and gray and manifested. This air sultry,
And once again a pale greening
Among the still-bare oaks and pecans.
I'm back east in the mind.
Back east in time with dogwoods,
With sweetgums. Time itself
Bent like the old river, a river
Apart from time and flooded with song.
Time itself just an application,
Meaningless, linear
Only to those linking arms and lining up
To cross over to some far shore.
But just look at young Daddy
Gathering arrowheads
In that ploughed bottomland field.
And look at young Mother
On the other side of the highway shelling peas
On the porch. I am a part of the equation,
Yet not of this world. I am a single note
In the song of the river.
A middle C, let's say, having sounded
And sounding and still sustaining
And hanging up in the rafters
In that great hall of this moment.

Soon Afterwards

I wake to find the crepe myrtle in color,
Each leaf a sunset, a flame flickering.
Morning air scented with yesterday,
With long ago and never again.

Morning air and the light it contains.
Morning air with its music of the dead.
It seems I'm much too late

For whatever is waiting for me
On the other side of the tracks. Whatever
They call it in the sweet bye-and-bye.
A mother's voice, her hands,

Her heart sung by the morning air.
Waiting beyond light, beyond long ago.
Waiting, fragile and forever.

Acknowledgments

Some of these poems have been published in the following journals, to whose editors grateful acknowledgment is given:

The Cape Rock: "Stranger in a Strange Land"
Fredericksburg Literary and Art Review: "Broken Arrow," "Caught by the Indian Summer Train," "Incidental Music"
Free State Review: "Colbert Mountain Sutra"
Good Works Review: "One Man's Purgatory," "Unsteady Lines," "Homesick Ballad in C Minor"
Jabberwock Review: "Ornithology 101"
Kestrel: A Journal of Literature and Art: "Epiphany in D Minor," "Suburban Ephemera"
Painted Bride Quarterly: "Alabama Field Holler"
typishly: "Vignette for Frank O'Hara"

"Never Enough to Go Around" and "Peacenik" first appeared in the anthology *Chicon Street Poets (Volume 1)* (Lit City Publishing, 2017).

Thanks, as always, to Ashley Savage Williams, Scott Alexander Jones, Robert Harrison, and Bryan Simmons for love, encouragement, and support. Also, much appreciation to Dennis Trombatore for his valuable input on this collection.

About FutureCycle Press

FutureCycle Press is dedicated to publishing lasting English-language poetry books, chapbooks, and anthologies in both print-on-demand and Kindle ebook formats. Founded in 2007 by long-time independent editor/publishers and partners Diane Kistner and Robert S. King, the press incorporated as a nonprofit in 2012. A number of our editors are distinguished poets and writers in their own right, and we have been actively involved in the small press movement going back to the early seventies.

The FutureCycle Poetry Book Prize and honorarium is awarded annually for the best full-length volume of poetry we publish in a calendar year. Introduced in 2013, our Good Works projects are anthologies devoted to issues of universal significance, with all proceeds donated to a related worthy cause. Our Selected Poems series highlights contemporary poets with a substantial body of work to their credit; with this series we strive to resurrect work that has had limited distribution and is now out of print.

We are dedicated to giving all of the authors we publish the care their work deserves, making our catalog of titles the most diverse and distinguished it can be, and paying forward any earnings to fund more great books.

We've learned a few things about independent publishing over the years. We've also evolved a unique, resilient publishing model that allows us to focus mainly on vetting and preserving for posterity poetry collections of exceptional quality without becoming overwhelmed with bookkeeping and mailing, fundraising activities, or taxing editorial and production "bubbles." To find out more about what we are doing, come see us at www.futurecycle.org.

The FutureCycle Poetry Book Prize

All full-length volumes of poetry published by FutureCycle Press in a given calendar year are considered for the annual FutureCycle Poetry Book Prize. This allows us to consider each submission on its own merits, outside of the context of a contest. Too, the judges see the finished book, which will have benefitted from the beautiful book design and strong editorial gloss we are famous for.

The book ranked the best in judging is announced as the prize-winner in the subsequent year. There is no fixed monetary award; instead, the winning poet receives an honorarium of 20% of the total net royalties from all poetry books and chapbooks the press sold online in the year the winning book was published. The winner is also accorded the honor of being on the panel of judges for the next year's competition; all judges receive copies of all contending books to keep for their personal library.

www.ingramcontent.com/pod-product-compliance
Lightning Source LLC
Chambersburg PA
CBHW070006100426
42741CB00012B/3124